IO117534

Charles Waddie

Historical Lessons on Home Rule

To which is added a Draft Bill for settling the whole Question

Charles Waddie

Historical Lessons on Home Rule
To which is added a Draft Bill for settling the whole Question

ISBN/EAN: 9783337158606

Printed in Europe, USA, Canada, Australia, Japan

Cover: Foto ©ninafisch / pixelio.de

More available books at **www.hansebooks.com**

HISTORICAL LESSONS

ON

HOME RULE;

TO WHICH IS ADDED

A DRAFT BILL FOR SETTLING THE WHOLE QUESTION.

BY

CHARLES WADDIE,

HON. SECRETARY SCOTTISH HOME RULE ASSOCIATION ;

AUTHOR OF "DUNBAR, THE KING'S ADVOCATE : A TRAGIC EPISODE IN THE
REFORMATION IN SCOTLAND;" "HISTORICAL INTRODUCTION TO
TREATY OF UNION BETWEEN SCOTLAND AND ENGLAND;"
INQUIRY INTO THE PRINCIPLES OF NATIONAL AND
LOCAL SELF-GOVERNMENT," ETC. ETC.

WADDIE & CO., EDINBURGH.
1887.

CONTENTS.

———————✦✦———————

THE
LESSON OF ANCIENT HISTORY.

——➤○◄——

T HE philosophical student of history, while taking a general survey of the record of events, may well be struck with dismay at the weary round of failures that beset the path of mankind in their efforts to set up a stable Government. The rise and fall of great empires seem to be regulated by laws over which the wisest statesmen and the truest patriots can have little or no control. Born of heroism and virtuous poverty, nations advance by slow and steady degrees till they attain to power and opulence, when the very success of their efforts brings about the vices that surely ends in their destruction. Is the record of past failures, then, to lead us to despair of setting up a Commonwealth that will alike meet the wants of a virtuous poverty and a time of luxurious wealth; or shall we not rather take the lessons of the past to heart, and, by wisely scanning the causes of destruction, steer the vessel of the State past the quicksands and rocks that have wrecked so many goodly navies, whose stranded hulls will serve as beacons to warn us of our danger?

The civilisation that prevailed in Europe and Asia before the advent of Christ, and for several centuries after, had little in common with the democratic or aristocratic Governments of the present day. The larger proportion of the inhabitants of these times were slaves— that is, were the personal property of citizens. These slaves, moreover, were not the negroes which are the only race who are bondmen in our day, but men of the same nation and blood as the citizens who owned them. Nor were these domestic slaves all born in the households of their masters, many of them had been free citizens who had become slaves through the misfortunes of war. War then, in these ancient times, was a more terrible calamity than it is even now, for the victorious army either put their prisoners to death or reduced them to slavery. In speaking of free and despotic States as applied to ancient history, it must ever be remembered that both forms of government had domestic slavery within their borders. In glancing, then, for a brief moment, at the state of society and the various forms of government that prevailed in the ancient world, we may be enabled to trace some of the causes of decay ; and, in taking a survey of the present state of affairs, see how far the lessons of antiquity are applicable to the circumstances of our day.

The countries whose shores are washed by the Mediterranean form nearly all that is known to us of the ancient world. The races of men who played the most conspicuous parts in the drama were the Greeks, Egyptians, Israelites, and Persians. Out of sight, however, the most prominent actors were the Greeks, who distinguished all other nations by the name of barbarians, not in the sense, however, that we apply to the word ; foreigners, perhaps, would more correctly express what was meant by the Greeks. Now, there were two forms of government which prevailed in the ancient world, the one the free republics of Greece, the other the complete despotism of Persia. The theocracy of the Jews, although so interesting to us, had litttle or no influence upon the public law of Europe. The Greek republics were small communities who, while not engaged in war with one another, had their valour amply gratified by the Persians and the other kingdoms that rose and fell in Asia Minor. The Greeks did not confine themselves to the limits of the country as now defined, but spread their colonies over those territories at present inhabited by the Bulgarians, Roumanians, and Turks; and moreover, they planted colonies on the shores of Italy, and took in the whole island of Sicily. Their form of government was admirably adapted for bringing out the full genius of the people; the free citizens could all take a part in the affairs of state, and they were kept in such modest limits that every man of note could be personally known to his fellow-citizens. There were no standing armies, as all had equal rights, every one was bound to military service in defence of the State. A vote of the people determined who was to be their general, and no one so honoured could decline to accept command, as witness Nikias sent by the Athenians, much against his will, to the conquest of Syracuse. Here, then, was a state of society the very antithesis of large kingdoms or great empires. Did the good that was done to mankind warrant their existence? Let us judge them by their fruits. The whole arts that adorn and beautify the life of civilised man took their rise from among these little republics. The dramatic muse, with its four great masters, Æschylus, Sophocles, Euripides, Aristophanes, rose to such a degree of splendour that some of the nations of Europe are to this day tied to the rules of art that regulated the productions of the Athenian stage. The epic muse, with its Homeric master, has never been surpassed. But need we detail the nine muses emblematic of the liberal arts that sprang from Greece? They are as familiar as household words. The virtues of a Socrates, the philosophy of a Plato, the eloquence of a Demosthenes stand out as eternal monuments of the virtues of free institutions, which alone can give scope to the divine nature of man.

Side by side with this busy intellectual growth, the little State of Israel was working out for mankind the everlasting doctrine of Monotheism, which was destined to break down the walls of superstition, and for ever free the human family from the degraded guidance of sooth-sayers, oracles and dreams. What we have gained by this freedom can best be understood by reading the lives of those bright spirits who were the kings of men. A peasant now would laugh at the fears that shook an Alcibiades, while an eclipse of the moon was sufficient to ruin the fortunes of an army in which Demosthenes was a general. While these free States were doing so much for mankind, the larger portion of the human family were under the dominion of a cruel despotism. The Persian Empire under Xerxes exhausted the country to minister to the pride and ostentation of a single man. His innumerable armies, his bridge of boats, his fleets which covered the sea, his gorgeous tents, his satraps whose armour was inlaid with gold, and the handles of their swords set with gems, his elephants with castles upon their backs, his eunuchs and his harems melted away before the genius of a Themistocles and the valour of a handful of free citizens. Again and again the hosts of Persia were broken upon the shores of Greece ; their riches and their greatness have passed away like a fan-tastic dream, while, amid the vicissitudes of fortune, the works of ancient Greece, and the products of her genius, rise to mock the ruins of time, and serve as guides to direct the artists of all succeeding ages.

The Phœnicians and Carthagenians were spreading civilisation along the shores of Africa, and showing forth the majesty of commerce. The Greeks were planting free states on the shores of Asia Minor. Many little nations were living a hopeful life in Italy, the founders of the great Latin race. The world was advancing steadily onward to a nobler state of society, when there appeared a cloud on the horizon not bigger than a man's hand at first, but destined to obscure the whole sky, and ultimately to put out the light of civilisation—the Roman Republic was born.

Whether the Roman Republic was originally founded by banditti, or that their enemies invented the story, it must be admitted that the career of that people gave a plausible colour to the invention. This congregation of outlaws, who founded a nation by committing a rape upon the Sabine women, conferred upon their offspring all the desire of appropriating other people's goods so common among brigands and other pests of society. True, the spoilation of their neighbours was upon a grander scale; the taking of a town and depriving it of its wealth and liberty is an heroic and glorious exploit, meriting the applause of mankind, while the taking of a purse from a passing traveller is a detestable crime. A true appreciation of ethical principles, however, will correct this partial opinion of the world, and declare that the depriving a people of their liberty exceeds in enormity any amount of recorded private crime. The world was now embarked in a struggle between universal empire and free national existence. The free states of Italy were the first victims to the insatiable greed of the Roman people. Then came the great struggle between Carthage and Rome, and happy would it have been for mankind if the former had been able to hold her own, and serve as a sufficient check to the growing insolence of the Roman people. The fortune of war went against Carthage, she perished; her history and her civilisation were ruthlessly destroyed, while the character attributed to her people was such as to reconcile mankind to the loss. The Romans declared that Carthage was unfit to live as a nation. This plausible excuse will be received by the philosopher with a certain amount of caution, for he will be slow to accept the character of a people from their enemies. The defeat of Hannibal and the destruction of Carthage left Rome without a rival. She was not slow to take advantage of her position, but at once set about the conquest of all the free states of Europe.

Every nation had to bow their head to Imperial Rome, the spoils of the world were brought to her, and, like other ill-gotten wealth, served only to degrade and corrupt her people.

The simplicity of manners which was the proud boast of the early Romans gave way before the tide of prosperity. Bribery became a common scandal of the day, and statesmen who held the foremost offices in the Empire unblushingly resorted to it. Degrading vices were openly indulged in, and to so low a point had the public morals fallen, that it is recorded of Pompeius, the idol of the people, not as a demerit, but something to be proud of, his intercourse with the courtesan Flora. Her statesmen were drawn from successful soldiers, and a corrupted people, ready for slavery, fell an easy prey to the first general who dared to march his soldiers into the streets of Rome. There was no longer any hope for freedom—the only matter to be decided was who was to be master. A crowd of soldiers contended for the bad pre-eminence of successfully destroying the liberties of their country. The ferocious Caius Marius, Sulla, Sertorius, Lucullus, Cæsar, and Pompeius were rivals in the inglorious war of ruining the Republic, while the virtues of a Cato were unable to rouse a people sunk in degrading vices, and gorged with the spoils of the civilised world.

Free institutions can alone flourish in a virtuous society; but the Romans had long got past that, and were fit only for a despotic ruler. The pride of a people sometimes outlives their virtue, so the emperors kept up the farce of a Senate to amuse the multitude, and delude the unthinking into the belief that they were a self-governing people. The decline of the Empire was the work of hundreds of years. Her degradation, which had its centre in Rome, spread slowly to Greece and Constantinople; for not even Christianity could arrest the terrible corruption that had taken hold of the civilised world. The Roman triumphs obliterated all feelings of generosity in the proud soldiers who took part in them, and in the people who witnessed the gorgeous, but cruel, spectacle. Pity for a fallen foe found no response in the breasts of the Roman people. The gladiator shows ministered to the savage instincts of our nature, while the shameless exhibition of debauchery upon the stage extinguished the last feelings of modesty that lingered in the breasts of both sexes. No longer a field for the display of the genius of the poet, the theatres were given over to actors whose lavish display of personal charms and loose gestures, dancers and buffoons, formed the daily amusement of the rich and dissolute citizens of Rome. The lascivious verses of Ovid broke down the modesty of the sexes, while Horace was not ashamed to prostitute his muse by praising a more odious vice, the practice of which is punished with death in every Christian country. A people steeped to the lips in vice, an army powerful alone against the liberties of the country, the victorious barbarians pressed upon Italy, and the Western Empire fell, and in its fall extinguished the light of civilisation.

When the seat of Empire was removed, Constantinople displayed the same odious picture of debauchery, varied only by the furious contentions of rival sects of religion, whose hair-splitting has been the scandal of the Christian faith. The amusement of the circus, where emperors wore the colours of the rival riders, showed to what a low level the public mind had fallen. Perhaps the Eastern Empire was all the more to be censured, for, being in the possession of the divine works of the ancient Greeks, she turned from the feast of immortals to feed upon the garbage of the theatre and the circus. Amid the general degradation of our race, we turn with pleasure to some bright examples of purity of manners; but even the heroic virtue of a Constantine Palœologus was unable to save the city from the furious soldiers of Mahomet. It fell also, and ushered in a long night of darkness for Europe, although from that storehouse of learning the seeds were scattered abroad which ultimately produced the revival of letters.

The lesson to be derived from this brief survey of the grandest chapter in the world's history, is that freedom cannot exist in one great centre. The wealth and corruption that is sure to flow to such a city will invariably destroy the purity of manners which alone can preserve public liberty. We have seen that the various small States that flourished in the ancient world raised the whole human family to a height of intellectual and moral grandeur that it had never attained to before. What would have been the position of Europe to-day if the various centres of intellectual growth had continued to do their work? we would have been as far in advance now of our present civilisation as we are from the time of William the Conqueror. The great blight of the Roman Empire destroyed all this: the imposition of her will upon all nations was the most terrible misfortune that ever fell upon the human family. Need we point the moral—Cherish small nationalities, it is there alone that true freedom and progress can exist, and the fullest measure of Home Rule alone can preserve them from the blight of centralisation.

THE
LESSON OF THE MIDDLE AGES.

———⟶∘⟵———

FTER the destruction of the Roman Empire,
Europe became a prey to various barbaric
hordes, and it would be impossible to
exaggerate the state of misery into which
the wretched inhabitants of once flourishing
countries had fallen. There was a saturnalia of
militaryism, where cruelty, rapine, and savage lust spread
ruin and dismay into every corner of the fertile provinces
of Rome. The teeming forests of Germany and the
populous shores of Scandinavia sent down horde after
horde into Gaul and Italy, and trod out the few remain-
ing signs of the refinement of life once so common
in these favoured lands. There was no regular form
of government, but each petty chieftain, count, marquis,
or duke, erected his castle, gathered around him a
few followers, and became the arbiters of the lives
and fortunes of the wretched inhabitants, who cowered
beneath the imperious mandates of those petty tyrants.

Amid this chaotic state of society, the various countries
which now form the European family of nations had
their birth. The very rudiments of political freedom
were unknown, the Government was the rule of the camp,
the arts of peace were despised ; learning there was none,
and the Jews, the only people who continued the

13

commerce of the world, alternately became the victims and the masters of these savage rulers. The successful general seized upon a country and proclaimed himself king ; he confiscated the lands of the people and parcelled them out among his servants, who, with the barbaric titles of earl, thane, marquis, count, or duke, imitated the pomp and circumstance of their master, and set up petty courts of their own, and divided the land out among their vassals. In this way were the modern kingdoms of Europe born ; and to such a height of arrogance did these princes attain, that, until recent years, they claimed for their power the special sanction of God¦; they were rulers by Divine right, and to resist any of their acts of tyranny was a crime against the Most High.

There was one common danger which knit together for purposes of defence the various races that were contending in Europe for mastery, and which overawed intestine faction. The rapid spread of the Moslem faith alarmed the Christians, and aroused their valour to make a supreme effort to check the victorious march of the soldiers of the Koran. That the success of Mahomet was arrested, is the turning-point of this dark chapter of human history; modern civilisation would have been an impossibility had the light of Christianity been extinguished. The struggle was a long and arduous one, and in its course, developed many new traits of character. The romances of the Middle Ages, with its chivalry and religious devotion, has been hallowed by genius, and adorned by the fairest offerings of art. What a sound policy failed to accomplish, religious fervour, stirred up by a fanatical priest, brought about. The successful preaching of Peter the Hermit, and the crusade which followed, will ever form one of the strangest and most romantic chapters in history. The flower of the youth of the West, impelled by an irresistible enthusiasm, laid down their lives upon the burning sands of Palestine ; and such was the infatuation of the times, that some of the most profligate of men died fighting for a religion which, during their whole lives, they had trampled upon. The strain upon the resources of Europe was terrible, the struggle for possession of the holy places in our eyes seems contemptible, but it was suited to the times; it kept the Moslems at home, and prevented the barbaric customs of the East from being the rule of life for the West. The success of Godfrey of Bulloigne, and the kingdom he established in Jerusalem, are important factors in the history of the world, while it is no small gain to mankind that this expedition to the Holy Land called forth the muse of the immortal Tasso.

The struggle of the great nobles to preserve their privileges from the encroachments of the king was the first break in the cloud of darkness that hung over public liberty. The old feudal barons disdained restraint, they were not subjects, but the king's good cousins and kinsmen, and exercised full authority over their vassals. The monarch was a ruler but in name; they joined his standard, at the head of their own vassals, when called upon to prosecute a war, for war was the business of their lives, and the architect of their fortunes. The king had only one resource from the overbearing insolence of the peers, and that was to grant charters to the burghers and craftsmen, who are a necessary element in all forms of society. They served as a buttress between the crown and the barons, strengthened the Government of the day, and ultimately enabled the king to reduce the nobles to the degree of subjects, and brought society into some form of order. It took centuries to accomplish this, during which there was almost continuous war, domestic or foreign. Agriculture was reduced to the most rudimentary forms, and the misery of the great body of the people seems to us almost incredible. Nominally there were no slaves, but in reality the vassals of the great barons suffered the most cruel forms of slavery, their lives, possessions, and the honour of their wives and daughters were subject to the caprice and lust of the dweller in the lordly castle.

A people so rude and barbarous became a ready prey to superstition. The little learning that remained in the world was the exclusive property of the Church, her priests alone could overawe the barons by appealing to their fears, while the remorse that ever follows upon dark deeds enabled them to enrich the Abbeys that were plentifully scattered over the land. The rise of the Papacy, and the enormous power it wielded over the rulers of Europe, is one of the most curious and instructive chapters in the world's history. The travesty of Christianity, the pagan rites incorporated into the creeds the profligacy of the clergy, the monstrous assumption of power over the temporal as well as the spiritual lives of the people, fills us at this distance of time with astonishment. Yet it is impossible, while censuring the Church for its many shortcomings, to forget the immense good it did during these long years of mental darkness. The light of science and art was kept alive in their religious houses, and any one inclined to learning found there the means of research and study. The civil as well as the canon law were expounded by her priests; bishops were chancellors; and the Universities grew under the fostering care of the fathers of the Church. The lands dedicated to the service of religion were always the most fertile, and her vassals the most opulent. In these evil times the Church, with all her imperfections, did a great and good work by making the revival of learning possible.

While the land was a prey to the violence of the barons, tempered only by the sway of the clergy, the sea was infested with pirates who reproduced, in an aggravated form, the evils so prevalent on the land. All along the shores of the Mediterranean lake these pirates had their strongholds. The tempests of the sea was the least dread of the merchant; a voyage was an adventure to be taken at long intervals, and when successfully accomplished, generally made the fortune of the hardy mariner.

The pirates did not confine themselves to the mere plundering of the vessels, the crews and passengers were taken to Algiers and sold as slaves, where a ready market was always found for Christians of both sexes. Impunity made them bold—fleets of swift sailing and well-armed galleys kept company, and made descent upon the land and carried off the trembling inhabitants. Many a Christian maiden spent the remainder of her days in the harem of some Turkish or Moorish Pasha, and to the other evils of their lot was added the bitterness of being compelled to adopt the hateful rites of Mahomet. The Christians made many a gallant fight at sea; and in one of these, the illustrious Cervantes was captured and made a slave. Fortunate it is for Spain that he was able to escape and write his " Don Quixote."

While the general state of society was one of violence, the private morals of the people were of the most depraved description. Low and cruel amusements, sensual pleasures of the basest kind, tales and songs reeking with obscenity, superstition, which took the savage form of torturing witches, bitter animosities and feuds, mean and cowardly revenges. To take off your enemy by poison or by the hired dagger of the bravo was a recognised institution of society. The public morals of Christendom look now with horror upon the private bravo; happy would it be for mankind if it would look with equal horror upon the public bravo. It is a sad reflection upon our Christianity that we have still in our midst men who hire themselves to do the bidding of any corrupt Government—standing armies who will march and crush out the life and freedom of any people at the will of their masters.

The darkness and horror of the European States was at length broken in Italy. The world began again the work of raising the human family from the brutish ways into which it had fallen. A number of little republics sprang up: Venice, Genoa, and Florence. As in the days of the Greek republics, the forms of society which prevailed in these little states served to nurse the genius of man, and gave forth a light which ultimately led to the present advanced state of civilisation. Venice gave dignity and power to commercial pursuits; and became so successful at sea as to be able to dispute the mastery with the Turks, and wrest from them some of the islands they had formerly conquered. The refinements of life were cultivated in their safe retreat on the Adriatic; and the proudest kingdoms in Europe considered it an honour to have these merchant princes as their allies.

To Genoa the world is indebted for the illustrious Christopher Columbus, and if that little republic had done no more for mankind, it would have entitled her to their eternal gratitude; but she was an honourable rival to Venice, and materially advanced the civilising process that ever follows upon legitimate commerce. When we turn to the Republic of Florence, we find a reproduction of the intellectual activity of ancient Athens. The solemn grandeur of Dante's divine comedy, the fascinating, yet profligate works of Boccaccio, which have had such an immense influence upon modern literature, the subtile penetrating genius of a Machiavelli, and the wealth of art which clustered around the De Medici, made that period an honourable rival to the age of Pericles. Lodovico Sforza, Duke of Milan, had sense enough to see that his court was honoured and his fame assured by the presence of Leonardo da Vinci. To the small state, of which Ferrara was the capital, we are indebted for the birth of modern epic poetry. The genius of Ariosto, so little appreciated by the prosaic Cardinal Ippolito, and the great work of Tasso, to which we have before alluded, are what we owe to this little principality.

It was impossible amid the blaze of light which the revival of letters produced that the superstitions of the Church, and the corruptions which had almost obliterated the Divine doctrines of Christ, could long escape the penetrating genius of the times. The Reformation—of which Luther, Melancthon, and Calvin were the leading spirits—was the blessed result of this new awakening. The spirit of inquiry was set in motion, and the Church only covered herself with ridicule in the forced recantation of Galileo. The march is steadily onward, and the researches of a Darwin and a Huxley will enable mankind better to understand the ways of God. Europe, shortly after the Reformation, was again exposed to a great danger. The discovery of the New World, and the influx of wealth that flowed to Spain, gave her such a commanding position in the world as almost to put her into the place of ancient Rome. Happy it is for mankind that her military genius fell below her opportunity. The destruction of the Armada and the triumph of the Dutch Republic averted so dire a calamity. The rapid rise of the kingdom of Spain, the wealth that flowed to her, reproduced in Madrid the vices that brought about the destruction of Rome, and with a like result. The remorseless wars of Cortes and Pizarro annihilated the civilisation of Mexico and Peru, while the spoils that flowed to Spain as the result of these wars corrupted her people. The debauchery of Madrid, the public corruption of the governing classes, and the remorseless bigotry of her Church, where the Inquisition in vain tried to stifle the truth by burning the best sons of Spain, but only succeeded in ministering to the savage instincts of our nature in the same degree as the gladiator shows of ancient Rome, brought about the fall of Spain. The insignificant position which that country now holds is an instructive lesson to the great kingdoms of the world. When freedom of thought and purity of manners are absent from a state, its fall is not far off.

The lesson to be drawn from this brief outline of the history of the Middle Ages is, that the world must stand still while great military states are contending for mastery; that little states are the chosen homes of genius ; that centralisation is not only a crime against national life, but against mankind in general. History repeats itself. As in the ancient world, the little republics did everything for mankind, so the revival of letters, and the march of progress which marks the greatness of the present day, is due to states which, judged by their numbers and wealth, are contemptible. Let the inhabitants of these Islands rejoice, then, that they have four distinct nations in their midst. The cherishing of these by a far-reaching, comprehensive system of Home Rule will be the best safeguards against the destruction of liberty, which ever dogs the steps of great empires.

THE
LESSON OF THE BRITISH EMPIRE.

THE contemplation of the vastness of the British Empire, its riches and power, its teeming population, and the variety of productions and climate that owe allegiance to one sovereign, is well calculated to make our breasts swell with emotions of pride. When we consider that this colossal state—greater than any known to ancient or modern history—has been built up in little more than one hundred and fifty years, we may well be struck with the energy and good fortune of the race that has subdued so large a portion of the world's surface. Compared with the British Empire, Rome in her palmiest days was a small state. Our Indian Empire alone contains a larger population than ever was subject to Rome, Carthage, or Greece; while our vast colonies, scattered over the whole earth's surface, are such as never entered into the wildest dreams of all the Cæsars and Ptolemys of the ancient world. Is this empire, then, like Jonah's gourd, which rose in a night, to perish in a night? A hundred years is a small chapter of time in the history of a great people. It is given to few men or nations to bear sudden good fortune with wisdom. Perhaps it would not be amiss then to consider our vast possessions and see how far our actions are calculated to produce stability, and promote the welfare of the vast aggregate of human beings that are intrusted to our care. The subject naturally divides itself into two halves—The conquests of Great Britain; and, The Colonies. We will take the former first.

In the year of our Lord 1704 the English took that gigantic fortress, Gibraltar, and have retained it ever since; but it was during the latter half of the eighteenth century that the true conquests of Britain began. In Europe the territory of this country has rather diminished than increased. The kingdom of Hanover was once a possession of the British Crown, but was peaceably surrendered when Her Majesty accepted the crown of Great Britain and Ireland. Yet it is a strange coincidence that the debt incurred by this country in defence of Hanover —the Marlborough wars, which were mainly waged because of our Continental connection—did not follow the kingdom lost fifty years ago, but remains a charge upon the British tax-payer to this day. It is not in Europe, however, but in Asia we must look for the conquests of this country. The East Indian Empire, which dwarfs all our other conquests, was founded by Lord Clive and Warren Hastings. The East India Company, of which these were but the servants, had no higher aim than to enrich themselves by the legitimate arts of commerce, and it was only accidental circumstances that set them on a career of conquest.

The evils that necessarily fall upon a country when ruled despotically were rampant in Bengal and the other states of India. A weak, cunning, and revengeful ruler deluged his court with blood, or some successful noble, equally cruel and remorseless, cut off the reigning family, and when possessed of superior energy, for a time knit together the loose elements of society and held firmly the reins of government. Then followed a period of prosperity and peace, during which the people grew rich and prosperous, to be followed by a season of crime and disaster at the death of the ruler. In an evil day, during one of these periodical upheavings of society, the weak monarch took it into his head to interfere with the commercial interests of the East India Company, and, coming in contact with a race of superior energy, gave them an opportunity of overthrowing the native government and reigning in its stead. The poor sons of Asia were no match for the European, even in cunning and duplicity. The battle of Plassy, the first great victory of the British, was the type of many a battle fought since ; we allied ourselves to a traitor to his native prince, who was only made a convenient stalking horse for our own usurpation. The eternal intrigues of an Oriental court were taken advantage of by these cool calculating traders of London, while the breaches of faith, small slips at the best, were remorselessly taken advantage of, to strip the prince of his dominions and the natives of their liberty.

Visions of boundless riches excited the cupidity of the people at home, and every needy adventurer took service under the Company with but one object in view—to make his fortune as quickly as possible, and return to his native land, and flaunt his ill-gotten wealth in the eyes of his admiring but envious countrymen. These adventurers were a race by themselves, and were called Nabobs. The wealth they possessed, and the vulgar display they made of it, completely turned the heads of the people of this country, who thought they had got possession of boundless riches. It is only within recent years that the truth has come home to us, that India is a poor country, poor in a sense unknown to Europe, so poor that we can hardly realise how human nature could hold together under such conditions of society. Humanity shudders when it thinks how fortunes were made out of such abject poverty.

The conquest of the native states so fortunately begun at Plassy went steadily on ; the process was simple but effective. Some frontier squabble brought demands for satisfaction, and when these were not instantly complied with, an army was sent to dethrone the reigning prince and put the head of the opposing faction, a friend of the British, upon the vacant throne. This creature of our own had imposed upon him a resident at his court, who was virtually his master, and who regulated all things after a European standard, and totally disregarded the wishes and prejudices of the people among whom he lived. Quarrels ensued, an excited crowd insulted the majesty of the British flag, the puppet king was dethroned, and a proclamation in the *Gazette* announced the fact that another kingdom had been added to her Majesty's dominions. Or trading companies spying some advantage in a native state, cajoled the prince into some concession or charter, the purport of which in all human probability he never understood, but, like a child grasped at the immediate gain, and when that was spent withdrew the concession. Complaints were made to the Governor-General of the wrong done to British subjects, peremptory demands for satisfaction were made, which were as peremptorily refused, the native Prince naturally thinking he was master in his own dominions. A sharp war ensued, and another kingdom was added to the crown. New swarms of adventurers arrived from Europe to administer the affairs of each fresh conquest, and make their own fortune—the most important of all administrations. Missionaries of the Gospel of Peace came to preach humility and righteousness to the perplexed Asiatic. Cathedrals and churches were erected out of the spoils of the native states, where the pale-faces were not to be disturbed in their devotions by the presence of niggers, as they politely described the descendants of the oldest civilisation in the world.

While we were busy conquering nations, the necessary public works for the storage of water, that all-important factor in the harvests of India, were neglected. The Mogul rulers were more humane and wise, but then they adopted the country as their own, and did not abide there for a season. The rains failed, as they have always failed periodically, the gaping earth devoured the crops, for the ruined water-tank held no water. Famine, with his gaunt visage, stalked over the land, and millions of our fellow-creatures laid them down upon the burning earth and died—the victims of the neglect of their foreign rulers. The resources of the country, which were bound-less, could not be brought to alleviate the distress in the famine-stricken provinces for want of the proper roads. Thus plenty, yea superfluity, might be in one province a few hundreds of miles away, while multitudes were perish-ing of want in another. The railways, the sole good given to the natives of India by their rulers, were laid down more with a view to the military occupation of the country than to the development of her resources. The cost of producing these iron roads was enormous, and the debt imposed upon so poor a country served still further to deepen the distress of the peasant farmer.

The evil effects of a corrupt system have a tendency to increase, and, in our own day, there has been a new development of cruelty and rapacity in our dealings with Asiatic states. We pick a quarrel with the Afghans, march into their country, take their capital, dethrone their prince, and call all who oppose us rebels. Who made them rebels to the British Crown? Is our own word to be the sole law of nations? Generals acted upon these infamous proclamations, and executed their prisoners in cold blood, and, instead of the butchers being tried for their lives as they ought to have been, Parliament thanked them for their services and rewarded them by rich donations and titles of honour, and, lest their tender feelings should be outraged by hostile criti-cism, the liberty of the native press was destroyed. Without a shadow of excuse, we are at present engaged in a war with Burmah, and, like a parcel of brigands, rob the palace of its jewels and crown, while the brave defenders of their native country we declare to be rebels and dacoits, for we are ingenious in inventing names to give us an excuse for our acts of usurpation. The provost-marshal, with a barbarity that sent a thrill of horror throughout the civilised world, took photographs of the dying agonies of the poor wretches who were executed for the crime of defending their native country.

To bolster up this heritage of blood we enter into criminal wars nearer home. The national party in Egypt must be suppressed, Alexandria levelled with the dust, the brave Soudanese slaughtered by thousands, and crime upon crime heaped upon our guilty heads to cry aloud to God for vengeance, which is sure to come upon us unless a speedy repentance stays the hands of Nemesis. The people in these islands have only in a very modified degree been responsible for the actings of their government in India. It is only within a few months that their own enfranchisement has been accomplished, giving them full control over the actings of their servants, and at the same time full responsibility for the deeds done in their name. India pays no tribute to this country, the taxes of the British workman is not reduced one farthing by contributions from Asia. It is a class and a class only of our fellow-countrymen who benefit from our Indian Empire. The government of so vast a territory requires the labours of a whole army of civil and military servants, who, paid at an extravagant rate, grow speedily rich, and return to their native country to live in idleness and luxury. It is not our purpose to inquire into the subject of whether the money spent in this country by these retired servants of India is a gain or loss to our population; that would be a curious and instructive study to the political economist, all we are concerned with at present is to point out that the mass of our population get no immediate gain from the conquests of our aristocracy.

From this sickening picture of depravity and wickedness we turn with particular delight to the contemplation of our Colonial Empire, which is the glorious production of the people of these islands, and perhaps it would be as well to pause for a moment to consider the grandeur of the first of these colonies, for although no longer legally connected with our country, the United States of America is truly a child of our own, whose proud position among the nations must ever give us the liveliest satisfaction. The Puritan Pilgrim Fathers, who sought a new home on the shores of America, and raised up the New England states, were the product of the religious persecutions that preceded and followed the days of the Commonwealth. Nursed in the principles of constitutional liberty, their character hardened by persecution, and with just that dash of superstitious fanaticism that makes men "Scorn delights and live laborious days," no body of men were better fitted to be the founders of a great nation. Lest there should be anything wanting, the English, with that blind fury that not unfrequently directs her rulers, sent troop after troop of her best sons, banished from their native land, to the American plantation for daring to assert the rights of man to equal justice and equal laws. The insane arrogance of the Home Government, which prompted them to impose upon such a people, taxes without representation, in the light of subsequent history is an event rather to be rejoiced over than lamented, for, although it may ruffle our national pride, it brought about the glorious declaration of independence of 4th July, 1776. The world then beheld the birth of thirteen new republics. Perhaps no one then living ever dreamt of the political significance of that event. Little more than one hundred years has elapsed, and we now behold a mighty nation, or rather a family of nations, where the local and national life is being steadily built up. A country with a compact territory larger than Europe, a population greater than any single state in the old world, yet managed with the perfection of order by an army of 25,000 men; a country from which the smallest state in the world has nothing to fear; a nation that the despot at the head of a million of men dare not insult, is the grandest testimony to the virtue of free institutions that the world has ever seen.

Side by side with this colossal state stands our Canadian colonies, but how different is their history. While the United States of America have been rushing on at the speed of an express train, Canada has been marching at the slow pace of the carrier's waggon. Signs of revival have in recent years shown themselves, and, perhaps, at the present day there is little difference in the progress of the two countries; both alike have a railway stretching from the Atlantic to the Pacific, while boundless territories have been opened up in the far West. What was the agency that awoke this new life and started our Canadian fellow-countrymen on this career of progress? It dates from the time of the rebellion, and the subsequent granting of free representative government. A country that is not the master of its own destiny must ever be condemned to perpetual insignificance, without patriotism and without national hope.

The group of colonies that are settled on the shores of the Australian island again show the power of free institutions to develop the best instincts of the human mind, and to produce that ideal of perfect government, the greatest happiness to the greatest number. The rapid rise of these colonies, a worthy rival to the United States, is one of the glories of the mother country, who, learning wisdom from Canada, at once granted free representative government at the first demand of the colonials. New Zealand and the Cape of Good Hope again tell the same story, while the only colonies that are drooping are those that are managed by the Crown Office in London.

Whether the dream of imperial federation with our colonies will ever be realised, or that each colony will set up an independent state of her own, will give little concern to the lover of mankind, whose only desire will be that the progress of the human family should be assured. The true glory of the British race is thus found in our colonies where the victories of peace have been achieved. Our battles have been with the wilderness, the advanced guard of our army has been the axe, clearing the forest, our battalions the plough, while the slain in our warfare is the grain that has fallen to the reaping hook. It has been declared in some quarters that there is no amount of deceit and cruelty that has been exercised upon the inhabitants of India to equal the barbarity that has been shown by the colonists to the feeble natives they have supplanted. This, if true, would be a foul stain upon the fair fame of our colonial fellow-countrymen ; but although in some cases there has been great inhumanity in dealing with savage tribes, it is not true that the general conduct of the European to the native races has been anything unbecoming a civilised people. The Indians in Canada, the blacks in Australia, and the Maories of New Zealand have been pining away since their contact with the white man, and their extinction cannot now be far off. This is not a consummation that has been devoutly wished for by our colonists; on the contrary, they have done all that lay in their power to arrest the decay of the native races. But there is a law above their benevolence as certain as the law of gravitation, and that is the survival of the fittest. As the native grasses of Australia wither and die before the stronger growth of the European plants, so the blacks fade before the sturdier sons of the old world. Races die of old age like individuals. Sentiment may drop a tear, compassion may stretch out a hand to the feeble race, but inexorable fate claims them for its own. The crust of the earth is made up of the debris of former races and former forms of life ; such are the ways of God, who can gainsay them ?

The lesson, then, to be derived from the contemplation of the British Empire is, that India being gained by the sword like other conquests, will fall away in course of time. It is no new experience in the history of India for it to be subdued by foreign races. Some have settled and got absorbed among the people, others, again, after a more or less lengthened sojourn in the country, have been expelled or conquered by some stronger power than their own. A little reflection must convince most men that this will ultimately be our fate. They who live by the sword will perish by the sword. But, before we go, it is to be hoped we will, as some atonement for the many wrongs we have inflicted upon that people, give them some lessons in the art of ruling the people by the people, and that the rudiments of constitutional government will be found in every province of India before our final expulsion.

Our colonies, however, need not these lessons, they have bettered the teaching of the mother country, and are in the proud position of being able to give us instruction. While England domineered over them, and tried to manage their affairs from London, there was no progress, but rather positive decay. Given the direction of their own affairs, they leapt forward with a bound. Would the same experience not be felt at home? Scotland, Ireland, and Wales drag on the weary journey of life with gyves on. Give them the mastery of their own destinies, and they will astonish the world, and redound to the glory of England, instead of, in the case of Ireland, being her shame.

THE LESSON OF LONDON.

IN the reign of Elizabeth, England was computed to have a population of five millions, while the only city of first-class importance, judged by our present standard, was London. This city was supposed by the provincials to have reached to prodigious proportions, yet it is doubtful if it contained as many inhabitants as the Edinburgh of the present day. If, then, we were to judge ancient London by the number and wealth of its inhabitants, we would form a very inadequate conception of its true greatness. But, during the wonderful reign of the Virgin Queen, the intellect and genius of the country rose to such a height of grandeur that no age before or since can be at all compared with it. London was the centre of this bright illumination, and although the revival of letters was somewhat later in appearing there than in Italy, and some of the other Continental states, it far exceeded any of them in the grandeur of the works of genius produced. It was not alone the dramatic muse that awoke the sympathies of a chivalrous people, yet in the great masters that then flourished, England overtops the whole world. The thundering verses of a Marlow, the quaint humour of Ben Jonson, the philosophic dignity of Shakespeare, and the easy gentlemanly carriage of John Fletcher, have so woven themselves with the genius of the language, as to make themselves indispensable studies to any one with pretensions to literary culture.   In other walks of the poetic art no less greatness was attained; the polished verses of Spencer, the delightful trifling of Herrick, are masterpieces of their kind.   The philosophic Bacon, the courtly Raleigh, Drake, and Dampier, each in their own walk found a home in London, and drew their inspiration from the court of Elizabeth and the pedantic James.

In so keen-witted an age it was impossible that the principles of government could long escape the eager scrutiny of the citizens of London.   The "Utopia" of the unfortunate More had already whetted an appetite for inquiry into political and social questions, and many schemes of model states appeared about this time.   The dissenters from the Church of England, the foremost Liberals then as now, imbibed constitutional forms of government from Geneva, and exercised them in ruling the various religious bodies that flourished in spite of the persecutions of the Church.   The fruit of this teaching appeared in the controversy between the Parliament and the King, unheard of doctrines were freely discussed, and appalled Europe beheld for the first time a monarch tried by his subjects for his life, condemned and beheaded; thus for ever shattering the doctrine of the divine right of kings.   The defence of the people of England by John Milton still further opened the eyes of Europe to the rights of man; while the power and prosperity of the Commonwealth clearly showed that a people could thrive without a king.   In all these controversies London took a foremost place. Her trained bands taught the Cavaliers to respect their valour, while constitutional government found eager supporters among her wealthy citizens.

Although there were occasional relapses, London steadily held on to Liberal political opinions, and in the press which flourished in the capital, the supporters of liberty and progress found its most ardent advocates. The provincial press drew its inspiration from London, and their proudest boast was that they were able to give the earliest notice of the opinions that prevailed in the capital. This was the state of affairs up to very recent times ; but let us pause now to consider the London of the present day.

In contemplating this wonderful city, the first thing that strikes us is its enormous size, containing within its bounds a larger population than the whole kingdom of Scotland. The magnitude of the city is alike its glory and its shame ; the advantages and disadvantages of urban life are put in sharp contrast. Boundless wealth reigning in one quarter of the city, with all the refinements of art and luxury directed by good taste ; and in another quarter, wretchedness and misery, degraded humanity in its worst form. The result of this familiar aspect of London is that no true bond of sympathy is found among the citizens, beyond the little circle of his own acquaintance no Londoner cares for his neighbour ; and it has been truly said of it, that nowhere in the whole world can one be so lonely as in London. The depressing effect of the weary miles of shabby streets, whose monotonous brick walls vie with each other in ugliness, tends to degrade the taste of the citizens, while the absence of the healthy air of the country and the thousand and one charms of natural scenery serve to lower the standard of intelligence of the dwellers in this great city. It is quite in keeping with this state of things that the most imposing buildings stuck at the corners of the streets are public-houses, or, in the local language, gin-palaces. There the sickly, feeble sons of London seek an artificial stimulant to give a fillip to their jaded faculties.

No truer index to the character of a people can be found than making yourself acquainted with their amusements. A wise countryman of ours said, " I care not who makes the laws of a country, it is the writer of songs who shapes the character of a people." If we then examine into the amusements of Londoners, we will not form a very high opinion of their intellect or virtue.

C

The dramatic muse has some forty houses dedicated to it, but with perhaps one exception, the pieces produced are only destructive of the taste or virtue of the people. The Government, with an astonishing want of wisdom, leaves this potent instrument for good or evil in the hands of private enterprise, whose only ambition is to make money, which experience tells them can best be got from protracted runs. The manager of a theatre then seeks for such pieces as will attract the greatest numbers, and again experience tells him he must seek a very low level of intelligence. To attract London, he must banish good taste, common sense, and pure morals, so the better an author writes, the greater the work he produces, the less are his chances of success. Inexperienced genius wastes many a weary hour dancing attendance upon the supercilious manager, wondering in his own mind how works so destitute of merit find a footing upon the stage, while his own finished productions are rejected. The countrymen of Shakespeare might well blush to find the London stage occupied with such pieces as the " Mikado," " Private Secretary," and " Pink Dominoes." But these pieces only show a lack of intelligence and good taste, others are not so innocent. In the so-called comic operas, we have a violation of good morals as well as good taste. Impossible scenes are put upon the stage, the bald chat occasionally lightened up with indecent inuendos, and gorgeously mounted. In these pieces the costumier and scene painter carry away the palm of excellence, but that nothing may be wanting to attract an idle and profligate audience, women dressed as nearly naked as possible, with lascivious glances and indecent gestures, stir up the passions of the pale-faced denizens of the pit.

In every depth there is a lower depth; the Lord Chamberlain has some check upon the theatre, little or none upon the music halls and dancing saloons. There vice, uncontrolled, revels in all its hideous deformity, the streets swarm with prostitutes, an army of procurers bring forward victims to fill the ranks thinned by disease and suicide. The wealth so copiously flowing into London from every quarter of the Empire is squandered by the most worthless of mankind. He who raises his voice against the prevailing vices is a marked man; woe unto him if he make any technical slip in the law : justice, asleep while the virgin tribute is being weekly paid to the Lotharios of London, rises with grim severity to punish the man who disturbs her respectable slumbers. The Divorce Court occasionally startles the country by its revelations. Those high in the land, rulers and statesmen, show another side to their greatness in the magnitude of their vices.

It has generally been considered an act of folly for a man to put all his eggs into one basket. If, then, this proverbial expression points to a real evil, what is foolish in an individual, cannot be wise in a State. Yet, this is what we have been laboriously aiming at for the last 180 years, sending everything to London ; that is, putting all our eggs into one basket. A number of thoughtful men, reflecting on our social state, have felt considerable alarm at the gradual depopulation of the rural parishes, and the rapid increase of our large cities. They maintain, and we think rightly, when towns reach a certain size, the population deteriorates, and a walk through the slums among the lapsed classes bears melancholy witness to the truth of their fears. If, then, this is so in towns like Glasgow, Liverpool, or Manchester, how much more it is the case with London ? Would not any scheme that would arrest its growth be a gain to the whole country ? Let us consider for a moment what this London is ; her population displays the sharpest contrast, the most unbounded wealth on the one hand, and the most abject poverty on the other ; the idle voluptuous luxury of the West End, and the degraded squalor of the East. This mighty city contains hundreds of thousands of criminals, and hundreds of thousands more constantly treading upon the skirts of meagre famine, a cesspool to receive the scoundrels of Europe. Its population are impulsive and foolish to a degree unknown to any other part of the country—now lashing itself into fury over the supposed wrongs of the Tichborne Claimant, or bewailing in gushing periods the loss of its Jumbo; all but coercing the Government into criminal wars, to gratify the so-called patriotic fervour of Jingo mobs, and so stretching the allegiance of the provinces to the snapping-point. This silly population, which is becoming more Tory every day, and consequently out of harmony with the prevailing sentiment of the country, has at its command unlimited wealth, unlimited material of war, unlimited field for recruits, and as if that was not danger enough, the public arsenals are entirely at their command, so that if at any time the capital and country should be of a different opinion, the capital has the means to overawe the country, and unscrupulous statesmen, hopeless of carrying the provinces with them, might find favour and power from London. If the teaching of history means anything, it points unmistakably to this great danger, all the greater that the general public are quite oblivious to it. The triumvirate at Rome stirred up the passions of the Plebeans, who, to revenge their Cæsar, washed out the liberties of the Republic in the best blood of her senators. In our own time, Napoleon III., by his Coup-d'Etat at Paris, made himself master of France, and established a corrupt despotism. Let it also be remembered that in Rome, under the Emperors, the farce of a Senate was maintained, and with mock solemnity the Conscript Fathers were duly consulted, and as regularly ratified the commands of the Emperor, while if there was any hesitation, a Sejanus was found who could quiet all opposition on the scaffold. Napoleon also found a way to reconcile universal suffrage with the most complete despotism. So our Parliament might be made to have all the constitutional forms and appearances of power without the reality.

The lesson to be derived from the contemplation of the present state of London is, that no greater menace to the liberty and well-being of Great Britain exists than her capital. The enormous size, the character of the people, which must, from the nature of things, become more enfeebled and depraved every day, points clearly to the duty, if the Empire is to be saved from its blighting influence, of taking as much of the business of the country out of it as possible. The granting of a full measure of Home Rule to the four nations forming the United Kingdom, would give a fourfold guarantee to our liberties. It might well also occupy the thoughts of Englishmen whether it would not be for the good of their country to remove their National Parliament to York, an older and a purer city than London, while the Imperial Parliament was retained in its old quarters. True patriotism and sound policy will be found in such measures as will cause the population of London to decrease. The removal of the public Arsenal from its immediate neighbourhood, and all Government work, would tend to put some restriction upon its enormous size; while the natural flow of wealth to the National capitals, and the numbers who must reside at the seat of Government, would naturally reduce the population of London. We know these proposals will be very distasteful to Cockneys; in the delirium of a fever we are not the best judges of what is good for us; the patient must swallow many a bitter potion or he will die.

What then is the moral of the whole book? We have seen in ancient history that great empires and large cities were destructive of liberty; in the Middle Ages that it was not the great monarchies that advanced the world; and also in the history of our own country, that the genius of our people flourished in its highest excellence when our population was small. This, then, is the whole matter : small states are chosen by God as the home of genius, and this can only be attained in Great Britain by dividing the country into four distinct nations, each with absolute power over its own destiny.

HOME RULE BILL.

THE following Act is professedly founded upon Mr. Gladstone's famous "Government of Ireland Bill," but is made applicable to the four divisions of the country, and, in our opinion, deals out equal justice to all, and is animated with a feeling of perfect trust in the people :—

A BILL TO AMEND THE PROVISIONS FOR THE DESPATCH OF BUSINESS IN GREAT BRITAIN AND IRELAND.

BE it enacted by the Queen's Most Excellent Majesty, by and with the advice of the Lords Spiritual and Temporal, and Commons in the present Parliament assembled, and by the authority of the same as follows :—

PART I.

LEGISLATIVE AUTHORITY.

I. On and after the first day of January, 1888, the Legislative Assembly for England shall consist of the Lords Spiritual and Temporal of England, elected as hereafter specified ; and the Commons, duly elected by the people of England, who shall have the exclusive authority over all private and public bills relating to that part of the United Kingdom called England.

38

II. On and after the first day of January, 1888, the Legislative Assembly for Ireland shall consist of the twenty-eight Lords Temporal of Ireland elected; and the Commons, duly elected by the people of Ireland who shall have the exclusive authority over all private and public bills relating to that part of the United Kingdom called Ireland.

III. On and after the first day of January, 1888, the Legislative Assembly for Scotland shall consist of the sixteen Peers elected; and the Commons, duly elected by the people of Scotland, who shall have the exclusive authority over all private and public bills relating to that part of the United Kingdom called Scotland.

IV. On and after the first day of January, 1888, the Legislative Assembly for Wales shall consist of the Lords Spiritual and Temporal of Wales, duly elected as hereafter specified; and the Commons, duly elected by the people of Wales, who shall have the exclusive authority over all private and public bills relating to that part of the United Kingdom called Wales.

V. The four divisions of the Parliament shall sit simultaneously in their respective countries; that is to say, the English in London, the Irish in Dublin, the Scotch in Edinburgh, and the Welsh in Carnarvon, to dispatch the business of each.

VI. Her Majesty shall summon the National Parliament to meet at such time for the dispatch of business as shall not interfere with their attendance on the Imperial Parliament.

EXECUTIVE AUTHORITY.

VII. The Executive Government of the four countries shall continue vested in Her Majesty, with the aid of such officers and such council as to Her Majesty may from time to time seem fit, but such officers and such council shall be different for each country, and have their offices located in the capital of each, and reside there during the sittings of the National Parliament.

VIII. Her Majesty shall give or withhold her assent to any bills passed by the national division of the Parliament as to her seems fit, in the same manner as she at present exercises her prerogative in the Imperial Parliament.

IX. Her Majesty may exercise her prerogative in summoning, proroguing, and dissolving the four National Assemblies, or any one of them, as to her seems fit ; but when she dissolves the Imperial Parliament, the National Parliaments by the same Act shall also be dissolved. But she may summon the Imperial Parliament without summoning the National Parliament ; in like manner she may summon any one of the National Parliaments, or any number of them, without summoning the Imperial Parliament. Moreover, it will be in the prerogative of Her Majesty to suspend the sittings of the National Parliament, and summon them to meet as an Imperial Parliament, in cases of peril, such as the imminence of war, or supplies for some sudden emergency.

CONSTITUTION OF LEGISLATIVE BODY.

X. The Imperial Parliament shall remain as at present. That is to say, a House of Lords and a House of Commons with full control over all Imperial affairs.

XI. The National Parliament of England shall consist of the present members of the House of Commons, sent by English constituencies ; and 104 Peers, elected by their own order, who will sit in one chamber, with equal votes. That is, each member, Lord or Commoner, shall have one vote.

XII. The National Parliament of Ireland shall consist of the 103 members of the Commons, and the 28 elected

Peers, who will sit in one chamber, with equal votes. That is, each member, Lord or Commoner, shall have one vote. Any Irish Peer, not sitting as a Peer in the Imperial Parliament or the National division, may sit as a Commoner if duly elected.

XIII. The National Parliament of Scotland shall consist of the 72 members of the Commons, and the sixteen elected Peers, who will sit in one chamber and have equal votes. That is, each member, Lord or Commoner, shall have one vote. Any Scotch Peer, not sitting as a Peer in the Imperial Parliament or the National division of the same, may sit as a Commoner if duly elected.

XIV. The National Parliament of Wales shall consist of the thirty members of the House of Commons, and seven elected Peers, who will sit in one chamber, and have equal votes. That is, each member, Lord or Commoner, shall have one vote.

POWERS OF THE EXECUTIVE AUTHORITY.

XV. The executive authority of each of the four countries shall have the full control and patronage of every office and act pertaining to that country, as at present enjoyed by the executive authority of the Imperial Parliament, except that which pertains to the raising of a revenue for Imperial purposes, as hereafter defined, and the army, navy, and diplomatic service.

XVI. Her Majesty may, by order in council, from time to time, place under the control of one or any number of the four National Governments, for the purpose of that Government, any such lands and buildings in the country referred to, as may be vested in, or held in trust for Her Majesty.

FINANCE.

XVII. For the purpose of providing for the public service of each of the four countries before referred to, the legislature of each country may impose direct taxes, which shall be collected along with, and by the same officers as the Municipal and County taxes; and the Imperial Government shall abstain in all time coming from imposing Property Tax, House Duty, and Land Tax.

XVIII. On and after the first day of January, 1888, there shall be a Consolidated Fund for each of the four countries, separate from the Consolidated Fund of the Imperial Government. All taxes imposed by the National Parliament of the four countries shall be paid into their respective Consolidated Fund, and be appropriated to the public service of each country according to law.

XIX. Custom and Excise duties shall only be imposed by the Imperial Parliament, and the moneys derived therefrom paid into the Imperial Consolidated Fund. Income Tax, Stamps, and the Post-Office shall continue as heretofore to form part of the Imperial Revenue.

Public Loans.

XX. All sums due for principal or interest to the Public Works Loan Commissioners, or to the Commissioners of Public Works, in each of the four countries in respect of existing loans advanced on any security in each of the four countries, shall on and after the first day of January 1888 be due to the Government of such country, and any Commissioners they may appoint shall have conferred upon them all the powers enjoyed by the present Commissioners.

For the repayment of the said loans to the Consolidated Fund of the United Kingdom the Government of each of the four countries shall be held responsible both for repayment of capital and interest in the manner and terms of the contract.

IRISH CHURCH FUND.

XXI. All rights over and all obligations to the Irish Church fund shall be transferred to the Government of that part of the United Kingdom called Ireland.

JUDGES AND CIVIL SERVANTS.

XXII. All judges and magistrates shall be appointed to their respective offices by the Government of each of the four divisions of the United Kingdom, and can only be dismissed from their office on petition to the Parliament sitting in the country in which their duties lie, and subject to the approval of Her Majesty.

The civil servants of the Crown, other than those employed in the collection of the Imperial Revenue, shall be subject to the Government of the country in which they serve, and shall be liable to be dismissed or retained as may be found expedient for the service of said Government.

POWERS RESERVED TO THE IMPERIAL GOVERNMENT AND PARLIAMENT.

XXIII. The national divisions of the Parliament may not raise an army or navy, give grants to volunteers, interfere with the succession to the Crown, enter into treaty with any foreign state, declare disabilities for any religious opinion or remove the conscience clause in the Education Acts, confer rights of citizenship upon foreigners, or alter the law of copyright, patents for inventions, trade marks, and other powers referred to in the Patent Acts, or alter the coinage of the realm.

COURT OF EXCHEQUER.

XXIV. The Court of Exchequer shall continue to be under the control of the Imperial Government, and the National Parliaments may, if they see fit, submit all causes relating to their revenue to the decisions of such Court. or appoint any other Court to deal with their own revenue. But in no case shall they interfere with the judges appointed by the Imperial Government.   All the powers at present exercised by the Court of Exchequer in Imperial finance are reserved.

POLICE.

XXV. The police force within the bounds of each country shall be under the control of the Government of that country who may as seem to them fit take charge of them or leave them to be regulated by the Burgh and County Authorities within each country.   The police shall not be armed and drilled as soldiers.

TRANSITORY PROVISIONS.

XXVI. The provisions contained in the 1st, 2nd, 3rd, and 4th schedules to this Act enumerating the Acts of Parliament, and other duties applicable to the four divisions of the country, shall be of the same effect as if they were enacted in the body of the Act.

XXVII. Schedule 5 shall contain a list of those Acts of the Imperial Parliament applicable to the four divisions of the country with the servants employed in enforcing the same, and shall state those that are alterable by the National divisions of the Parliament and those that are reserved for Imperial control.   The servants employed in enforcing the Acts that are alterable by the National divisions of the Parliament shall be paid by and subject to the Government of that nation.

APPLICATION OF PARLIAMENTARY LAW.

XXVIII. The Parliament of each of the four countries forming the United Kingdom may frame such rules for regulating debate and the procedure of business as to them seems fit, subject to the approval of Her Majesty in Council.

DEFINITION OF IMPERIAL AND NATIONAL AUTHORITY.

XXIX. Should there be any dispute as to the respective powers of the Imperial authority and the National Governments, then the merits of such dispute shall be referred to a committee of members of the four divisions of the Parliament, equal numbers of each, and a proportionate number of Lords from each country, whose decision shall be final, subject to the approval of Her Majesty in Council.

www.ingramcontent.com/pod-product-compliance
Lightning Source LLC
Chambersburg PA
CBHW021557270326
41931CB00009B/1260

* 9 7 8 3 3 3 7 1 5 8 6 0 6 *